PAPER FOLDED
FLOWERS

First published in Great Britain 2017

Search Press Limited
Wellwood, North Farm Road,
Tunbridge Wells, Kent TN2 3DR

Text copyright © Elizabeth Moad 2017
Photographs by Paul Bricknell at Search Press Studio
Photographs and design copyright © Search Press Ltd 2017

ISBN: 978-1-78221-426-7

The Publishers and author can accept no responsibility for any consequences arising from the information, advice or instructions given in this publication.

Suppliers

For details of suppliers, please visit the Search Press website: www.searchpress.com

You are invited to the author's website: www.elizabethmoad.com

Publisher's note

All the step-by-step photographs in this book feature the author, Elizabeth Moad, demonstrating paper folding. No models have been used.

Printed in China through Asia Pacific Offset

Acknowledgements

Many thanks to Beth Harwood and the whole team at Search Press for producing such a fantastic book. Thank you to Paul Bricknell, photographer, for all his patience and support!

A big thank-you to the great manufacturers of all the great tools and papers available for our creativity: Sizzix for the Big Shot die-cutting tool; Kaiser Craft, Echo Park, Basic Grey, Graphic 45, The Japanese Shop and many others for their amazing papers.

Finally, thank you to all the crafters around the world for sharing the love of all things paper!

ELIZABETH MOAD

PAPER FOLDED

FLOWERS

SEARCH PRESS

Contents

OCCASIONS

Greeting card
18

Gingham rosette card
22

Valentine's Day card
26

Springtime gift box
30

Get-well gift bag
34

New baby gift bag
38

Mother's Day card
42

DÉCOR

EVERYDAY

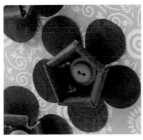

INTRODUCTION

Paper holds a fascination for us from an early age: we use it creatively in our childhood, and as adults, it surrounds us both at work and at home. When given a leaflet, paper ticket or notelet we tend to bend, curl and generally fiddle with the paper, unable to keep it flat! This book seeks to harness those temptations to use paper creatively, to make flowers using a variety of folding methods.

In crafting terms, papercrafting refers to the art of using paper and card as a basis from which to work, to make greeting cards, keepsakes and decorations. Other crafts are brought into the mix such as layering, cutting, punching, stamping and, of course, folding. This book features an array of folding techniques, from the simple to the complex, to create a range of flowers and floral motifs. From easy concertina folds to more complex sequences of folding, photographic steps guide you through each process.

Essentially, you need only paper or card and a few basic tools with which to get started with paper folding. This book is divided into three sections for easy reference, based on the purpose of each project, starting with **Occasions** (from page 18), then **Décor** (from page 48) and finally **Everyday** (from page 74).

Templates are provided throughout the book to help you with the projects. However, I hope that the ideas and techniques presented in this book inspire you to create your own designs and launch off in your own direction!

In today's frenzied world, where calm is ever more frequently sought out, papercrafting provides a simple and enjoyable method of relaxation, and eases stress. By taking time out and focusing your attention away from the hubbub of daily life, you can be productive and gain a sense of your own achievements. If you then give an item that you have personally handmade to a friend or family member, you are sharing the love of papercrafting even further!

PROPERTIES OF PAPER

Paper, paper, paper – everywhere we turn! As crafters, we are naturally drawn to the pretty printed papers sold in craft stores, which are of a high quality and often embellished with attractive designs. However, if you keep your 'paper radar' switched on, you will often find other wonderful sources of inspiration. How many of us have saved a stash of used wrapping paper for 'something special'? We can see old cinema tickets, stubs and all kinds of paper paraphernalia in a new light, and find ways to use them within our crafting world. On these two pages, we explore what makes paper and card such valuable assets to crafting.

Size

Paper is sold in many sizes. Common sizes are 297 x 210mm (11¾ x 8¼in), known as A4, 420 x 297mm (16½ x 11¾in) or A3; US letter or legal sizes are typically 279 x 216mm (11 x 8½in) or 356 x 216mm (14 x 8½in) respectively.

Scrapbook paper sizes are usually 203 x 203mm (8 x 8in) or 305 x 305mm (12 x 12in), or sold in pads of varying sizes. Origami paper squares come in a variety of sizes depending on the supplier – the most common are 75 x 75mm (3 x 3in), 150 x 150mm (6 x 6in) or 205 x 205mm (8 x 8in).

Wrapping paper, both manufactured and handmade, comes in a variety of sizes, again depending on the supplier, in single sheets or on rolls.

Greeting card blanks – pre-scored and folded sheets of card, some with apertures already cut out – are sold at sizes ranging from 90 x 90mm (3½ x 3½in) to 205 x 205mm (8 x 8in), in rectangular or square format.

Weight

Understanding the weight of paper or card is not straightforward: the weight does not refer to each individual sheet but to the thickness and sturdiness of a larger, whole sheet.

The following are general guides for weight of paper and card:

Lightweight	between 80 and 120gsm (54 to 81lbs)
Medium-weight	between 120 and 150gsm (81 to 101lbs)
Heavyweight	between 150 and 200gsm (101 to 135lbs)
Greeting card blanks	between 250 and 300gsm (135 to 203lbs)

Grain

Another important feature of paper is the grain, as found in wood. Working with the grain means that the paper will tear in a relatively straight line. Working against the grain means that the paper will be harder to tear and will have a much more uneven edge.

Texture

The surface and texture of paper vary greatly: it might be shiny, bumpy with a 'hammer' finish, or with a linen-type texture. It might also be embossed, where parts of the surface are raised, or foiled, where parts of the design are enhanced with a metallic layer.

Suitability

Paper that is expected to have a short life span will be acidic and therefore will turn yellow, become brittle and deteriorate quickly. If you are making a keepsake that you would like to last a long time – perhaps years – then it is important to choose acid-free paper and cardstock. This means that the lignin (a bonding element that holds wood fibres together) has been removed during the paper production process, and the paper will last much longer if kept in good conditions.

All paper will fade in direct or bright sunlight; a greeting card left on a windowsill will soon discolour. This may not be a problem if you choose to make a bright, colourful card, but do be aware that cards exposed to sunlight will only have a short life.

Care and storage of paper

As a papercrafter you will build up a collection of tools, papers and general bits and pieces; the bad news is that you have to store it somehow! Collecting paper for future projects is a great habit so that you have a wide choice at your fingertips – but don't let it take over!

1. Try to keep papers flat – if they are kept upright they will buckle and bend. Keep them clear of objects that may squash or crumple papers.
2. The atmosphere of your work area is important. Always store paper out of direct sunlight, and keep it away from possible sources of damp.
3. Be aware of the potential fire hazard of paper stock. Make sure you have smoke alarms in your workroom and keep a fire blanket handy.

YOUR BASIC TOOLKIT

When taking on any new craft for the first time, it is useful to stock up on the basic tools and equipment with which to get started. This basic toolkit consists of items that will be of use for any project in this book.

If you are an established crafter it is useful to review your kit regularly, and update or renew essential pieces. This is particularly important for scissors and craft knives as these gradually become blunt, and we do not notice!

⌃ Craft knife

A craft knife is ideal for cutting straight edges and should always be used on a cutting mat, against a metal ruler. Always keep a sharp blade in the knife and change the blade regularly.

⌃ Pencil and eraser

Use an HB pencil to mark lines on papers and to trace templates.

Large scissors

Small scissors

⌃ Scissors

Small, fine pointed scissors are ideal for cutting out delicate areas. A second, larger pair of scissors always comes in handy for bigger sheets of paper. Keep all scissor blades sharp and clean.

⌃ Metal rulers

Use a metal ruler when cutting with a craft knife: a cork base prevents the ruler from slipping. A small metal ruler without a cork base is useful for scoring and measuring.

▷▷ Cutting mat

A self-healing cutting mat is essential. When cut with a knife, the edges of the cut come together again, or heal, so as not to leave an indent. The lines marked on the mat can be used as cutting guides to save you time measuring. Mats also protect your work surface from glue and scissor marks. Do be aware that a cutting mat can only cope with vertical or horizontal cuts – angled cuts will gouge the surface of the mat.

⌃ Tweezers

Fine-tipped tweezers are useful for picking up and positioning tiny embellishments such as self-adhesive gem stones. Some tweezers are self-locking so you do not need to keep them squeezed.

⌃ Bone folder

This smooth, flat tool can be used to smooth creases and strengthen folds.

⌃ Needle tool

This tool has many uses such as making holes for inserting brads, or for applying a tiny amount of glue.

⌃ Double-sided tape

This narrow tape can be used for mounting paper or card with more accuracy than glue.

⌃ Glue

Water-based, all-purpose glue, such as PVA, which becomes transparent when dry, is suitable for most papercrafts.

⌃ Cocktail sticks

Cocktail sticks can be used to apply small dots of glue to paper for delicate work.

ADDITIONAL TOOLS

Some of the projects featured in this book use specialist tools as shown on these two pages. These tools make certain techniques easier and less time-consuming. However, my philosophy is to purchase the items in the basic toolkit initially, and accumulate more specialist tools over time.

⌃ Die-cutting tool

Die-cutting tools give a cleaner cut, in any size or shape, than scissors or punches do. Place a shaped metal die on top of your paper and sandwich both between two sheets of clear acrylic plastic on the conveyor. Turn the lever to run the die under the rollers in the central unit for a neat cut.

⌃ Scalloped-edge scissors

Used in the same way as normal scissors, these produce a scalloped cut instead of a straight line.

⌃ Fringing tool

This tool slices paper in narrow, 90° cuts, to give a fringed edge. Move the lever up and down to feed the paper through the tool.

⌃ Quilling tool

This quilling tool has two thin prongs at its tip, between which quilling paper is threaded. When you turn the handle, the paper coils into a spiral.

⌃ Adhesive foam pads

These small pads are great for achieving a raised effect when you are attaching flower motifs or embellishments to your work. Foam pads are adhesive on both sides.

⌃ Buttons & adhesive gem stones

Simple embellishments such as these can be sewn or stuck onto your work for a final, decorative flourish.

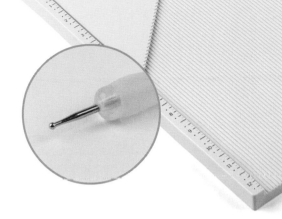

▷▷ Scoring board and scoring tool

A scoring board is a plastic board with evenly spaced grooves, to fit a sheet of paper or card up to 305 x 305mm (12 x 12in). A scoring board is typically used in conjunction with a scoring tool (see inset), which has a small ball tip that fits into the grooves to make scoring easier (see page 14).

Alternatively you can use a creasing tool for sharper scores: this is a flat instrument with a blunt, pointed tip. I use the creasing tool on pages 58 and 70.

⯯ Craft punches

If you do not want to invest in a die-cutting tool, there are many circular, shaped, or scalloped-edge punches available to crafters. They work like a regular office hole punch, and can be used on paper or card to make neat shapes.

To minimise paper wastage I work with the punch upside-down to position it as close to the previous cut-out circle as possible; however, for the purposes of this book, all punches are shown with the lever uppermost.

Punches can jam and stick with a lot of use. You can punch through waxed paper to loosen the punch but do not use oil. Punches will become blunt over time: to sharpen them, punch through kitchen foil.

Left, circle punches: 16mm (½in) and 25mm (1in) in diameter.

In this book, a variety of different-sized circle punches and dies are used, ranging from 16mm (½in) to 60mm (2¼in) diameter. However, you can work with the tools you already have, and use the items stated in each project as a guide only.

Small and large heart punches

Craft punches are available in all shapes and sizes. The punch below produces a circle with a scalloped edge.

TECHNIQUES

Folding

Clean scores and folds make all the difference to producing neat, finished items. Our eyes are very quick to pick up faults and whilst we are home crafters, ultimately we still aim for a professional finish.

There are two types of fold: valley and mountain. In a valley fold, the crease is at the bottom of the paper and the sides fold upwards – the shape is a 'V'. In a mountain fold, the crease is at the top, and the sides fold downwards. The shape is the exact reverse of the valley fold, and resembles a mountain.

Scoring

A score is a line indented into paper or card; the line then becomes a folded edge. The paper or card is not cut through scoring. Scoring allows accurate folding, prevents cracking and crinkling, and produces a neat crisp fold line. You will not need to score every fold; however, it does make a difference and can soon become habit.

To use a scoring board and tool, place the paper on the board and run the scoring tool over the paper, along a chosen groove. Press downwards with the tool all the time you are scoring.

Scoring a fold

▶ **STEP 1**

Start by making two light pencil marks where the score line is to be. Place the metal ruler along the line to be scored, cork side down to avoid the ruler slipping.

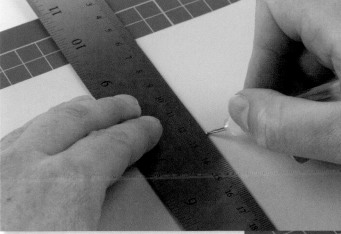

◀ **STEP 2**

Hold the ruler firmly in place. Run the scoring tool against the edge of the ruler, pressing down firmly on the tool. The scoring tool needs to compress the fibres of the paper along the intended fold.

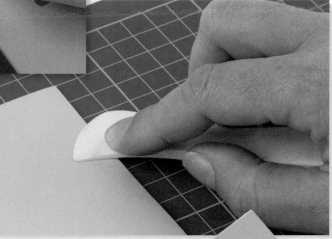

▶ **STEP 3**

Remove the ruler. Fold the paper all the way over at the score line. Run the bone folder along the folded edge, pressing it down gently.

▶ **STEP 4**

Open out the paper and make a score line along from the first. Fold the paper in towards the existing fold and smooth it with a bone folder. Open out the paper once more to reveal both a valley and a mountain fold.

Tip

You can turn the ruler over and line up with the score line, then fold the paper over the ruler to maintain the straight fold.

Mountain fold

Valley fold

Cutting

Often in papercraft projects, an author will suggest using scissors or a craft knife to cut out. This advice is fine for an experienced crafter; however, a newcomer to papercrafts may not have the knowledge to support their choice of cutting tool. Personally, I have found that it is not possible to cut a long, straight line using scissors, however large they may be. The only way to guarantee a perfect straight line is to use a craft knife, cutting mat, a metal ruler – and a steady hand!

Some crafters use a guillotine – I generally do not, as I prefer the greater control afforded by a ruler and a knife. However, you may find a guillotine a useful tool.

If you are not used to using a craft knife, practise before you make a decisive cut, as you will need to co-ordinate both hands. Even now, my ruler will slip when I am cutting if I do not focus fully on what I am doing.

Tips

- Always cut paper with the section you want to use under the ruler; if the knife slips, it will cut into the waste section.

- Stand up when cutting at a work desk with a knife. That way, you can put more pressure on the metal ruler to hold it in place and stop it from slipping.

- If you do choose to use scissors, they need to fit comfortably in your hand while you hold the object to be cut in the other hand. Move the paper as you cut, and keep the scissors stationary.

Cutting a straight line

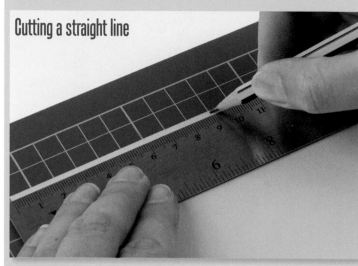

▲ **STEP 1**

Use an HB pencil and a metal ruler to mark out two points at the top and bottom of the sheet if you are cutting a small piece of paper, or three points – with one in the centre – if the paper is larger.

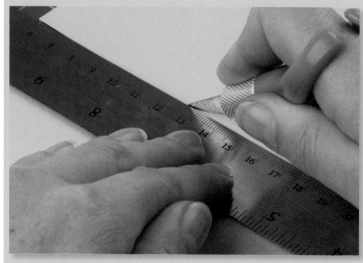

▲ **STEP 2**

Place your metal ruler along the line to be cut. Then place the blade of the knife at a 45-degree angle next to the ruler at the top of the paper. Draw the knife towards you, keeping it flat against the ruler. Use a single movement to cut the paper. If you are cutting a large sheet, cut approximately 200mm (8in) down, then, keeping the knife in the paper, move your other hand down the ruler and press firmly down before you continue to cut.

Before you remove your hand from the ruler, it is a good idea to run the craft knife along the cut once more to ensure it is fully cut through and along. Remove the ruler and the paper should fall apart.

Glueing and sticking

It is important to use the right adhesive for the job. Very often I see attendees at my workshops applying PVA glue to large areas of paper, then wondering why the paper cockles. PVA glue makes paper soggy as the water content of the glue warps the paper.

It is best to use a glue that is labelled 'tacky' or 'high-tack'. This means that the glue is typically thicker and has less water content. The high-tack element means that the glue will be strong and will dry quickly.

On larger areas of paper, use double-sided adhesive tape, combined with a few dots of PVA glue at the corners if it is needed.

For small areas, decant a small amount of PVA glue onto aluminium kitchen foil, and apply it to the paper using a cocktail stick or needle tool. Do not apply the glue straight from the pot, leaving the lid off, as this will dry out the whole pot.

Note

PVA glue is easy to wash off hands and equipment, but if applied in large quantities to paper, it will make the paper soggy and wrinkled. Glue sticks – which are tubes of solid glue – are good for applying an even coat of adhesive that will not make the paper soggy.

Occasions

Greeting card

Create a pretty and striking greeting card in fresh colours using easy punching and folding techniques. Handy paper punches take the effort out of papercraft and help you achieve a professional finish. Cutting out perfect circles by hand is not only hard but also takes a huge amount of time, which is why punches are such an asset to papercrafters.

Here, we use punched circles to make a three-dimensional flower design.

The finished card.

Materials and tools

▷ Basic toolkit (see pages 10–11)
▷ Floral patterned paper, 300 x 300mm (12 x 12in)
▷ Cream card blank, 110 x 110mm (4¼ x 4¼in)
▷ Yellow ribbon, 400mm (15¾in) long by 3mm (⅛in)
▷ Die-cutting tool with 60mm (2¼in) round die
▷ Circle punch, 25mm (1in) diameter
▷ Clear gem stone, 3mm (⅛in) diameter

▲ STEP 1
Punch eighteen 25mm (1in) diameter circles from the patterned paper. Set aside one circle.

▲ STEP 2
Fold seventeen of the circles in half, pattern outermost.

▲ STEP 3
Glue one folded circle to the underside of the unfolded circle, which will become the base of the flower. Ensure that one folded point is at the centre of the base circle.

▲ STEP 4

Glue the remaining folded circles to the centre circle, each partially inside the opening of the folded circle on its left. Ensure all circles face the same direction and are spaced evenly apart to create a tidy, round shape.

▲ STEP 5

After you have tucked in the seventeenth folded circle to complete the flower, stick a clear, self-adhesive gem stone to the centre of the flower shape using tweezers.

▲ STEP 6

Cut a 100mm (4in) square from the patterned paper. Using a die-cutting tool, make a 60mm (2¼in) diameter round aperture in the patterned paper

▲ STEP 7

Attach the patterned paper, with aperture, to the front of the cream card blank, using double-sided tape.

Tip

When you stick a line of double-sided tape to paper or card, press down hard on the end of the tape so that it sticks to the paper surface. Then lift up the backing strip with a fingernail.

▲ **STEP 8**

Glue the flower shape in the centre of the aperture.

▲ **STEP 9**

Finally, tie yellow ribbon around the spine of the card in a bow, and trim to size.

Gingham rosette card

This double-layer rosette is a unique, graphic alternative to a traditional flower motif. Individual squares in different sizes are folded to make the kite shapes that form two rosettes. The smaller rosette fits on top of the larger one for extra pizazz.

Why not try making more rosettes from green or brown patterned papers?

The finished card.

Materials and tools

- ▷ Basic toolkit (see pages 10–11)
- ▷ Double-sided blue patterned card, 300 x 300mm (12 x 12in)
- ▷ White card blank, 180 x 130mm (7 x 5in)
- ▷ Light blue card, 160 x 120mm (6¼ x 4¾in)
- ▷ 2 x small turquoise brads, 3mm (⅛in)
- ▷ Circle punch, 25mm (1in) diameter
- ▷ Adhesive foam pad

▲ STEP 1
Cut blue patterned card into twenty-four squares: eight at 40 x 40mm (1½ x 1½in), sixteen at 20 x 20mm (¾ x ¾in).

▲ STEP 2
Score a light line diagonally across each square.

▲ STEP 3

Hold the square with the centre score line vertical in front of you. Fold one corner and edge into the centre line.

▲ STEP 4

Fold the opposite edge and corner into the centre line. The square now looks like a kite, with the two side corners meeting at the centre line.

▲ STEP 5

Fold the corners back on themselves to form a 'collar'.

▲ STEP 6

Punch a circle 25mm (1in) diameter from the patterned card. Glue the larger folded squares to the circle with the folded points in the centre.

◀ STEP 7

Repeat steps 2 to 6 for the sixteen small squares. Glue eight squares apiece onto a punched circle of patterned card 25mm (1in) in diameter, to make two small rosettes.

▲ STEP 8

Pierce a hole at the centre of the smaller rosettes with a needle tool. Push a turquoise brad through each hole and spread out the wings of the brad on the reverse side.

Tip

Brads are tiny wire clips with domed tops and two narrow, flat wings that fit through a hole and open out to fasten a paper item in place.

If you don't have a brad, use a gem stone or small button to complete the flower.

▲ STEP 9

Glue the large rosette directly to the rectangle of light blue card. Mount one smaller rosette on top with an adhesive foam pad.

▲ STEP 10

Stick the blue card to the white card blank using double-sided tape. Cut a strip of blue patterned card 6mm (¼in) and glue to the card, with the reverse pattern uppermost. Glue the second small rosette onto the strip to finish.

Why not make... a matching gift tag

Often when you complete a card project there is enough material left over to make another item quickly. Gift tags can be made in little time.

Make the rosette by folding eight 20mm (¾in) squares as seen in steps 2 to 4, but without folding the corners back into a 'collar' as in step 5. Pierce a hole in the rosette and insert a 4mm (¼in) blue brad to fasten. Attach the rosette to a circle of card 80mm (3¼in) diameter. Finally, pierce a hole in the circle and thread some pretty ribbon through.

Valentine's Day card

Paper-cutting has become popular recently with intricate designs producing amazing results. In this project, simple paper-cutting is combined with the folding of three heart-shaped flowers. Paper-cutting requires care and should not be rushed, but is a skill worth adding to your repertoire.

Materials and tools

▷ Basic toolkit (see pages 10–11)
▷ Pink card, 150 x 110mm (6 x 4¼in)
▷ Red card, 120 x 60mm (4¾ x 2¼in)
▷ White card blank, 180 x 130mm (7 x 5in)
▷ Pink patterned paper, 150 x 150mm (6 x 6in)
▷ Thin white copier paper for template
▷ Plain card for template
▷ Low-tack masking tape
▷ Double-sided tape

The finished card.

Templates

These templates are reproduced at actual size. Dashed lines indicate where to score to create a fold.

Template A

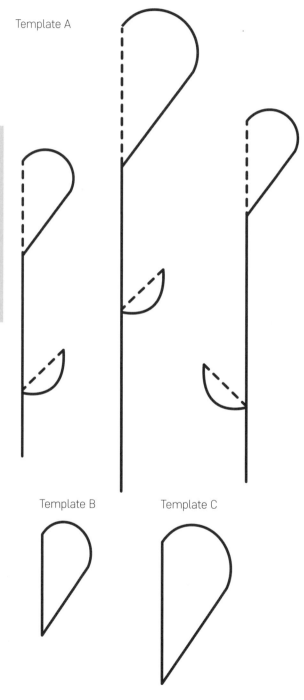

Template B   Template C

▶ STEP 1

Copy template A on page 26 onto thin white copier paper. Secure this with low-tack masking tape to the rectangle of pink card. Ensure that you attach the template to the reverse of the grain side of the card.

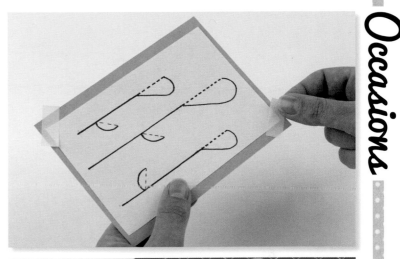

▶ STEP 2

Cut the pink card through the paper template along the solid lines only. You can use a ruler when cutting the straight stems.

▶ STEP 3

Remove the white paper template but keep it to hand for reference. On the pink card, score along the dashed lines indicated on the template for each of the flower shapes, and for each of the leaves.

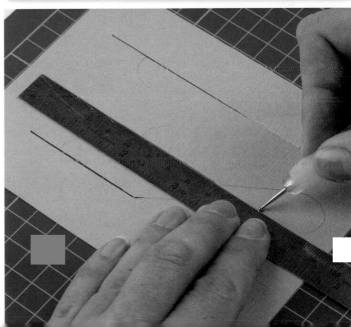

▲ STEP 4

Use a bone folder to fold back the pink card along each score line.

▲ STEP 5

Use templates B and C on page 26 to cut out two heart-shaped guides from plain card. Trace two large hearts and four smaller hearts (two hearts per flower) onto pink patterned paper folded with the pattern outermost.

◀ STEP 6

Use small scissors to cut out the heart shapes carefully.

▲ STEP 7

Use double-sided tape to attach the pink card to a rectangle of red card, with the petals and leaves folded outwards. Glue one of the large patterned hearts to the front of the large pink card heart.

▲ STEP 8

Then glue the second patterned heart to the reverse of the first patterned heart. Repeat for the two smaller flowers. Finally, tape the red and pink card to the white card blank.

Tip

Why not write a secret message on the flower petals?

Why not make... a gift tag

Use one of the smaller flowers from template A (page 26) to use as a guide. Follow steps 1 to 4 to transfer the flower silhouette onto a rectangle of pink card cut to 110 x 60mm (4¼ x 2¼in).

Attach the pink card to a rectangle of red card, cut to 145 x 70mm (5¾ x 2¾in), with the corners cut diagonally 20mm (¾in) down from the top edge.

Using template C (page 26) as a guide, cut two folded heart shapes out of patterned paper that matches or co-ordinates with your greeting card. Attach one heart to the lifted side of the pink card petal, and the second heart to the reverse of the first patterned paper heart, as shown in steps 7 and 8 of the main project.

Pierce a hole through the narrow edge of the red rectangle, and thread through some ribbon to complete the tag.

Springtime gift box

Spring is a time of growth and renewal in the natural world, and in using a fresh colour palette of green shades to make these three-dimensional flowers, we evoke that floral abundance most associated with that season.

The flower shown here comprises only four petals, but the teabag-folding technique used to create the petals gives the flower extra dimensionality.

These flowers would be perfect to use at Easter as a motif on a gift or card; however, they do suit any occasion!

The finished gift box.

Materials and tools

▷ Basic toolkit (see pages 10–11)
▷ Blue box with lid, 80 x 80 x 80mm (3¼ x 3¼ x 3¼in)
▷ 4 x sheets of green patterned origami paper, each 155 x 155mm (6 x 6in)
▷ 5 x pearl adhesive gem stones, 3mm (⅛in) diameter
▷ Die-cutting tool, 80mm (3¼in) diameter circle die and 60mm (2¼in) diameter circle die

▲ STEP 1
Use the die-cutting tool to cut four circles 80mm (3¼in) diameter from green patterned origami paper. Cut out eight circles 60mm (2¼in) diameter. Put the smaller circles aside for now.

▲ STEP 2
Fold a large circle in half with the pattern outermost.

▲ STEP 3
Fold the circle in half again.

▲ STEP 4

Open out the paper circle fully to reveal two sets of fold lines.

▲ STEP 5

Fold the circle in half again, this time with the pattern innermost, to create a third set of fold lines.

▲ STEP 6

Hold the circle with the patterned side uppermost. Push the side edges (valley folds) inwards, to form a hat shape.

▲ STEP 7

Place the shape flat on your work surface and gently lift up a folded segment with your fingers.

▲ STEP 8

Squash this segment down flat.

▲ STEP 9

Repeat for the opposing side. Make three more shapes in the same way following steps 2 to 9.

▲ STEP 10

Glue all four folded pieces to the lid of the gift box, with the points facing into the centre of the lid.

▲ STEP 11

Stick a self-adhesive pearl gem stone to the centre using tweezers for precision.

▲ STEP 12

Following steps 2 to 9, fold all eight 60mm (2¼in) diameter circles. Glue two shapes in a bow to each side of the box. Stick on gem stones to complete.

Why not make... a greeting card

Make a greeting card with a difference! Place two bold yellow flowers on a blue background – the complementary colours really 'sing' when placed together, and will bring cheer to the recipient of the card!

Make two flowers using petals in the two different sizes (80mm/3¼in and 60mm/2¼in). Assemble the flowers following steps 2 to 11 of the main project, and glue to a rectangle of blue card, 153 x 110mm (6 x 4¼in). Mount this on a yellow card blank 180 x 130mm (7 x 5in). Cut stems and leaves from the patterned yellow paper by hand and attach.

Finally, add a gem stone centre to each flower, and add a greeting if you wish.

Get-well gift bag

Making papercrafts to lift the spirits of a poorly friend or relative is a nice way to show that you care; and the recipient is sure to be cheered by these bright, folded flowers. As these particular flowers are made from heart shapes, this is an extra-special way to show someone that you are thinking about them.

Here, I have chosen two soft shades of mauve and green for a soothing colour theme.

The finished gift bag.

Materials and tools

▷ Basic toolkit (see pages 10–11)
▷ Heart-shaped paper punches in two sizes: 25mm (1in) and 16mm (½in)
▷ Circle punch, 16mm (½in) diameter
▷ 2 x sheets patterned, double-sided card, 300 x 300mm (12 x 12in) in mauve and green
▷ Gift bag, 190 x 150mm (7½ x 6in)

Templates

If you do not have heart-shaped punches, use the templates below:

▲ STEP 1
Using the larger heart punch, cut seven heart shapes from the mauve patterned card. Use the circle punch to cut out one mauve patterned circle.

▲ STEP 2
Fold the heart shapes in half vertically (using the point and the centre of the two curves as the folding line).

▲ STEP 3
Glue one folded heart to the circle with the point inwards. Glue the next folded heart alongside, making sure that the fold is on the same side as the first.

▲ STEP 4

Attach all seven hearts to the circle, taking care that they are evenly spaced. Ensure the shapes are touching but not overlapping.

STEP 5 ▶

Repeat steps 1 to 4 to make two more large flowers in the mauve card, and three large flowers in the green card.

▲ STEP 6

To make smaller flowers, use the circle punch to cut out a green patterned circle, 16mm (½in) diameter. Cut out seven hearts with the smaller heart punch. Use tweezers to attach the tiny petals to the circle with glue.

▲ STEP 7

Use a small dab of glue on the reverse of the circles to attach the flowers decoratively to one side of the gift bag to finish.

35

Why not make... a matching get-well card

Make a matching card to accompany the gift bag by using the same techniques as shown in the main project.

Cut a circle of purple card 100mm (4in) in diameter and mount on a mauve card blank 140 x 130mm (5½ x 5in). Attach a strip of green patterned paper along the bottom edge of the card. Make one large flower with green double-sided card and glue to the centre of the circle. Now add four green and four small mauve flowers around this, alternating the colours. Secure the card with ribbon, tied in a bow.

New baby gift bag

Celebrate a new addition to the family! The fancy flower on this sweet bag is made using simple folding techniques and a fringed flower centre. The birth of a new baby is a wonderful event, and when you spend time hand-crafting a gift, that gift becomes extra special.

When these scalloped-edge circles are folded, both sides of the patterned paper are visible, which gives the impression of a three-dimensional flower.

The finished gift bag.

Materials and tools

▷ Basic toolkit (see pages 10–11)
▷ Yellow gift bag, 160 x 120mm (6¼ x 4¾in)
▷ Scalloped-edge circle punch, 50mm (2in) diameter
▷ Pink floral, patterned double-sided card, 300 x 300mm (12 x 12in)
▷ Quilling papers: yellow, 3mm (⅛in) wide and pink, 10mm (⅜in) wide
▷ Quilling tool
▷ Fringing tool

Diagram

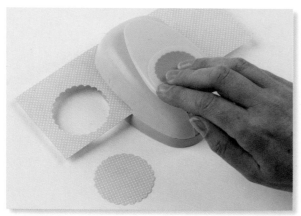

▲ **STEP 1**
Use the scalloped-edge circle punch to cut eight circles from the double-sided patterned card.

▲ **STEP 2**
Place each circle on a cutting mat, simpler patterned side facing up. Score four lines on the circle following the diagram above, using a scoring tool and metal ruler.

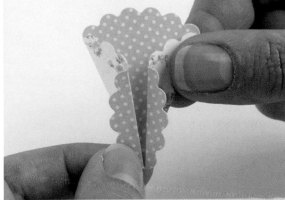

▲ STEP 3

Hold the circle so that the four scored lines 'meet' at the top. Fold score line **a** inwards, then fold score line **b** outwards again, creating a simple zigzag fold.

STEP 5

Repeat steps 2 to 4 for six of the remaining circles.

▶ STEP 6

Mark the centre of the unfolded circle with pencil. Glue each folded shape to this circle, narrowest end pointing in towards the pencil mark. Ensure that the folded shapes are equally spaced.

▲ STEP 4

Repeat with the opposing edges.

▲ STEP 7

Cut a 200mm (8in) length of pink quilling paper. Fringe with the fringing tool. Alternatively, cut narrow strips into one long edge of the paper by hand, with small, sharp scissors. Do not cut through the whole width.

▲ STEP 8

Glue the length of pink quilling paper to a 100mm (4in) length of yellow quilling paper so that half of the yellow length is still visible. Insert the end of the yellow paper between the prongs of the quilling tool.

◀ STEP 9

Coil the paper by turning the quilling tool away from yourself, and keeping the paper taut.

▶ STEP 10

When you reach the end of the length of pink paper, glue the end in place, then remove the quilling tool.

Tip

To save time, you can skip the fringed flower centre and attach a cute button in place here instead.

▲ STEP 11

Spread out the pink fringe with your fingertips to create a flower.

▲ STEP 12

Glue the completed flower to the yellow gift bag. Finally, glue the fringed centre to the flower.

Why not make... a card for a baby shower

At the time of a baby shower, the gender of the baby is not always known, so give a card in pretty, neutral colours instead.

Make the flower following steps 1 to 6 of the main project, using green double-sided patterned card and make the fringed centre from yellow and green papers following steps 7 to 12. Pierce a small hole in the wide edge of one petal and thread through a short length of yellow ribbon.

Make a 100mm (4in) round aperture in a yellow card blank (150 x 125mm/6 x 5in) using a die-cutting tool. (Note: many craft suppliers sell cards with pre-cut apertures so you can use these if you prefer not to cut your own apertures.)

Finally, tie the flower to the card so that it hangs in the aperture.

Mother's Day card

This pop-up card folds flat to post, then opens into a seven-flower bouquet – a beautiful explosion of colour!

    This card may seem complex, but once you have mastered the techniques involved in constructing the bouquet, this project is sure to become a firm favourite.

    I used bright pinks, yellows and oranges for maximum impact; however, a bouquet of a single colour can look equally effective.

Materials and tools

▷ Basic toolkit (see pages 10–11)
▷ Green card (for base), cut to 140 x 220mm (5½ x 8¾in)
▷ 4 x sheets of paper, 297 x 210mm (11¾ x 8¼in): orange, yellow (two shades), pink
▷ Felt pens: yellow, orange
▷ Plain card for template

Note

You will need to make two pink flowers, two orange flowers and three yellow flowers, of which one should be cut out of a darker shade of yellow paper.

Template

This template is reproduced at actual size. A dashed line indicates where to score to create a fold.

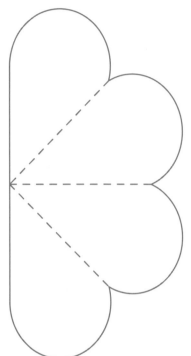

▲ STEP 1

Make a cardboard guide from the template on this page. Cut each coloured sheet of paper in half vertically, then fold in half. Draw around the template above, lining the long edge against the fold of the paper.

▲ STEP 2

Cut out each flower using small, sharp scissors.

▲ STEP 3

Fold the flower in half horizontally to make a heart shape, ensuring that you match up the curves of the petals.

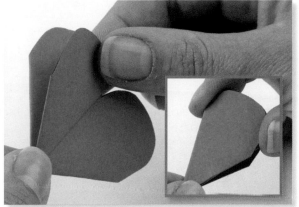

▲ STEP 4

Fold one quarter of the shape back on itself, to form a concertina petal shape (see inset).

▲ STEP 5

Open out the flower again, revealing eight folded segments. Cut out one segment and discard it.

▲ STEP 6

Fold the flower in half with the missing segment toppermost. Lay the flower face down. Overlap the two petals either side of the cut-out segment. Glue these together, ensuring the shape will fold flat. The flower now has six segments only. Repeat steps 3 to 6 for the other six flowers.

◀ STEP 7

Keep all flowers folded in half. Place a light yellow flower on your work surface, with the point facing you. Apply glue to the tips and edges of the petals. Attach an orange flower on the left-hand side of the yellow flower, and a pink flower to the right-hand side. Make sure all the folds line up.

◀ STEP 8

Glue the darker yellow flower on top of the three already glued together, with the point facing you.

◀ STEP 9

Glue the second pink flower on the left-hand side of the darker yellow flower as shown. Glue the second orange flower to the right-hand side of the darker yellow flower.

▶ STEP 10

Finally, glue the remaining yellow flower on top, with the point facing you, as shown. Put the flowers to one side to allow the glue to dry.

▲ STEP 11

Starting 10mm (½in) in from either short edge, score the green rectangle of card across its width at 50mm (2in) intervals. Fold and crease the score lines using a bone folder.

▲ STEP 12

Cut a line 80mm (3⅛in) down the central score line. Turn over the card and fold back two flaps either side of the cut to form a 'collar'. Use the bone folder to make the folds crisp.

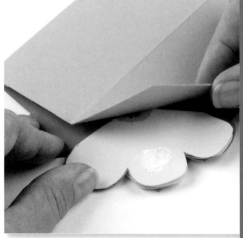

▲ STEP 13

Fold the card base back on itself (keeping the 'collar' outermost). Glue or tape one edge flap inside the other. Open out the card to form a box (see inset).

▲ STEP 14

Unfold the flowers and, with the yellow and orange felt-tip pens, colour the centres of the three yellow flowers, which should sit at the front of the formation.

▲ STEP 15

Once the ink has dried, fold up the flowers, and glue them to the green card, attaching the outer petals to the two collars to complete. As the glue dries, ensure that the card will lie flat but will also open out easily.

The finished card.

Décor
Orchid arrangement

Create these intricately folded flowers for use as a table centrepiece – they are sure to be admired.

Paper flowers are a wonderful home decoration, and by making your own you can choose colours that will harmonise with your décor. These orchid-like flowers are inspired by *kusudama*, Japanese origami flowers.

The number of petals can vary from flower to flower: for this project, the red flowers have three folded petals each and the orange blooms have five petals each.

Materials and tools

▷ Basic toolkit (see pages 10–11)
▷ Red and orange papers, 297 x 210mm (11¾ x 8¼in)
▷ Floristry wire, white
▷ Rubber stamp (floral peg)
▷ Ink pad, red
▷ Scrap paper

Red ink pad and rubber stamp

▲ STEP 1
Cut out three squares of red paper 70mm (2¾in) each. Place these onto scrap paper. Using the floral rubber stamp and red ink, print and stamp all over the paper squares in a random pattern.

▲ STEP 2
Fold each square in half, point to point, with the stamped pattern outermost.

▲ STEP 3
Run the ink pad along the open edges of the shape.

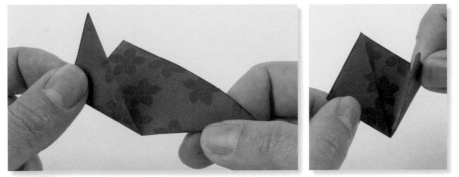

▲ STEP 4

With the fold horizontal and the point at the top, fold both bottom corners upwards and in towards the top point. Crease each fold.

 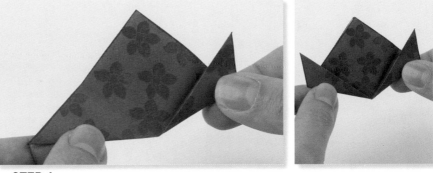

▲ STEP 5

Open out the two folds.

▲ STEP 6

Keeping the long edge horizontal and facing you, fold the right-hand corner up to meet the crease you have just made on the right-hand side. Do the same for the left-hand side. The two points will now extend over the outer edges of the shape.

◀ STEP 7

Gently fold the overlapping corners over the edges of the shape.

▲ **STEP 8**

Using a cocktail stick, apply glue to one of the uppermost triangle folds.

▲ **STEP 9**

Bring the other side in to meet the fold, and form a cone. Hold the sides in place whilst the glue dries. Then push down the small inner folds to create a stamen. Repeat steps 2 to 9 to create two more red petals.

▲ **STEP 10**

Glue the petal shapes together by the short, flat areas.

▲ **STEP 11**

Thread a length of floristry wire through the centre of the flower. Apply a dab of strong glue to the tip of the wire, then pull it back down inside the flower so that it attaches to the flower. Be careful not to get glue on your fingers.

Tip

Flowers with five petals can be made in much the same way following steps 2 to 9. At step 10, five petals are glued together to make a larger flower.

▶ **STEP 12**

This completes the first flower. Make as many as you would like, to form a bouquet.

The finished arrangement.

Framed flower

Placing a large, single flower in a frame transforms it into a longer-lasting keepsake. This flower makes a pretty picture that could adorn a craft room, or make a gift for a friend.

Paper is scored, folded, then glued to construct the three-dimensional triangle shape. Twelve identical shapes are arranged in a circle to make the flower. The pearl gem stone in the centre adds a lustrous touch.

Materials and tools

▷ Basic toolkit (see pages 10–11)
▷ Plain card: pink, light pink
▷ Patterned double-sided card, 300 x 300mm (12 x 12in)
▷ Picture frame, 180 x 180mm (7 x 7in)
▷ Pearl gem stone, 10mm (⅜in) diameter
▷ Die-cutting tool (optional)

▲ STEP 1

From the patterned card, cut twelve squares, 40 x 40mm (1½ x 1½in), using a sharp craft knife and metal ruler for clean cuts. Score a line across the diagonal of each square with the ruler and scoring tool.

▲ STEP 2

Hold the square with the score line running vertically. Fold the side corners in to the centre score line, forming a kite shape. Crease the folds with a bone folder.

▲ STEP 3

Partially overlap the two folded sides to form a triangular opening. Apply glue between the overlapped edges. Hold the shape whilst the glue dries. Repeat steps 2 to 3 for all squares.

▲ STEP 4

Cut a circle of pink card 100mm (4in) diameter and make a pencil mark in the centre. Glue each petal shape to the circle with the tapered point at the pencil mark to create the flower.

▲ STEP 5

Tape the circle onto a square of light pink card 150 x 150mm (6 x 6in). Attach the gem stone to the centre of the flower. Finally, insert the flower, on card, into the picture frame.

Note

In the final photograph, the glass has been removed from the frame to make the flower stand out. However, the flower can also be placed behind glass in a box frame in order to protect the paper and card stock.

The finished framed flower.

Why not make... a gift tag

Follow steps 1 to 3 to create eight triangle shapes from 30mm (1¼in) pieces of double-sided patterned card. Glue the shapes onto a 60mm (2¼in) circle of dark pink card, spacing them out evenly. Mount the circle of card onto a larger, lighter pink circle card 80mm (3⅛in) in diameter. Finally, apply an adhesive pearl gem stone 10mm (⅜in) diameter to the centre.

Kirigami garland

Kirigami is a Japanese term for paper-folding and cutting, originating from the words *kiru* ('cut') and *kami* ('fold'). Most of us learn this technique as children when we make snowflakes for window decorations. The practice of folding paper, cutting and snipping it, then opening it out to reveal a snowflake is such a joy; we can apply the same principles here to make lightweight garlands.

Here, we use strong Japanese wrapping paper as it is the ideal weight and is easy to cut when folded.

This project can be scaled up to make larger flowers. Begin with larger squares of paper and follow the same instructions.

Template

This template is reproduced at actual size.

Materials and tools

▷ Basic toolkit (see pages 10–11)
▷ Sheet of red patterned Japanese wrapping paper, 760 x 530mm (30 x 20in)
▷ Plain card for template

▼ STEP 1

Cut five 100mm (4in) squares from the wrapping paper. Fold each square of paper in half point to point, with the pattern outermost.

▼ STEP 2

Lightly mark the centre line of the triangle in pencil, as shown in the diagram below.

▲ **STEP 3**

Fold the two outer corners over, across the centre line.

◀ **STEP 4**

Fold the whole shape in half vertically, edge to edge.
Press firmly with a bone folder to crease.

◀ **STEP 5**

Draw a pencil outline of
the template on page 54
onto the folded piece.

▲ STEP 6

Use small, sharp scissors to cut around the drawn template. Cut inwards from the longer outer edge.

▲ STEP 7

Open out the shape to reveal the flower.

STEP 8

Make as many flowers as you need for a garland and glue them together in a delicate chain. Vary the flowers by making small changes to the template at step 6.

The finished garland.

Why not make... a greeting card

Make two flowers from the wrapping paper, following steps 1 to 7. Prick a hole in the centre of both flowers with a needle tool, layer the flowers and push a small red brad (4mm/¼in) through both. Spread out the wings of the brad on the reverse side of the flower, and glue it to a yellow card blank, 160 x 130mm (6¼ x 5in). Now attach a 10mm (⅜in)-wide strip of the paper across the top of the card and a 25mm (1in) strip across the bottom.

Concertina flowers

These pretty flowers are constructed from four individual squares of paper folded in a concertina form, then folded in half and glued together.

Although surprisingly simple to construct, the flowers are bright and jazzy, and would cheer up a room or make a colourful centrepiece for a dinner party.

I have used patterned origami paper for this project; however, you can use any strong paper or pretty gift wrap.

The finished flower.

Materials and tools

▷ Basic toolkit (see pages 10–11)
▷ Origami paper, double-sided, patterned, 1 x orange, 1 x blue (each sheet: 205 x 205mm/8 x 8in)
▷ Wooden sticks (e.g. barbecue skewers) 240mm (9½in) long
▷ Scoring board and creasing tool
▷ 2 x gem stones: orange and grey-blue, 5mm (³/₁₆in) diameter
▷ Orange card
▷ Circle punch, 25mm (1in) diameter
▷ Strong glue

Tip

Attach the finished flowers to thin wooden sticks and arrange them in a small vase for impact.

▲ STEP 1

Cut four squares, each 100 x 100mm (4 x 4in), from the orange paper. Place each square on the scoring board, and, with a creasing tool, score across the diagonal from the top to the bottom point.

▲ STEP 2

Score every 5mm (³/₁₆in) either side of this central score line.

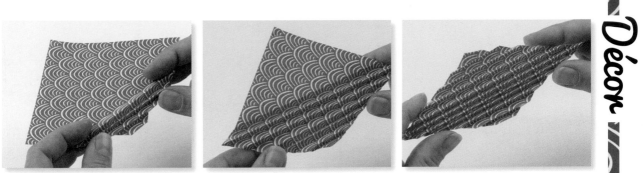

▲ STEP 3

Remove the paper from the scoring board. Starting from one corner, concertina-fold each square of paper against the score lines. Fold the paper back and forth until you reach the opposite corner.

▲ STEP 4

Bend the paper shape in half to form a 'v' shape.

▲ STEP 5

Glue the inside fold from the centre up by 30mm (1¼in). Pinch the inside folds together until the glue dries and the concertina shape resembles a double petal. Repeat steps 1 to 5 for the remaining three squares of paper.

◀ STEP 6

Glue all four petals together with the tips outermost and the fold of each at the centre.

▲ **STEP 7**

Cut or punch a 25mm (1in) diameter circle from plain orange card, and glue to the reverse of the flower. Attach a wooden skewer to the circle on the back of the flower with strong glue or narrow strips of tape.

▲ **STEP 8**

Add a grey-blue gem stone to the centre of the flower to complete. Repeat all steps to make similar flowers from contrasting blue patterned paper in 70mm (2¾in) and 90mm (3½in) squares. Stick an adhesive orange gem stone to the centre of each blue flower to finish.

Tip

Layer a smaller flower on top of a larger flower for a different effect.

Why not make... a greeting card

The purple and white patterned papers used here are 60 x 60mm (2¼ x 2¼in), creased and concertinaed as in steps 2 to 3, at 5mm (^{3}/₁₆in) intervals. For this project I have folded five double petals for a fuller bloom. The flowers are glued onto two layers of orange card (the darker card is 160 x 110mm/6¼ x 4¼in; the lighter card, 170 x 120mm/6¾ x 4¾in) and mounted on a white card blank 178 x 126mm (7 x 5in). Glue a 28mm (1in) wide strip of the purple patterned paper across the bottom of the card to complete.

Map bunting

Bunting has become very popular recently and is no longer just found outdoors; it is now a favourite indoor embellishment for parties and celebrations. Bunting can be made from fabric, felt or even wool – but it can just as easily and effectively be made using paper, card and matching ribbon!

For this project, I have cut scalloped circles from old road maps and folded them to form simple flowers. The flowers are then attached to five pennants of bunting; although you can make as many pennants as you need for a longer garland of bunting.

Materials and tools

▷ Basic toolkit (see pages 10–11)
▷ Scalloped-edge circle punch, 50mm (2in) diameter
▷ Scalloped-edge scissors
▷ Card, 297 x 210mm (11¾ x 8¼in): orange, three shades
▷ Paper map
▷ Orange brads, 5mm (¼in) diameter
▷ Orange ribbon, 10mm (½in) wide
▷ Orange sewing thread, doubled-up or double thickness
▷ Sewing needle

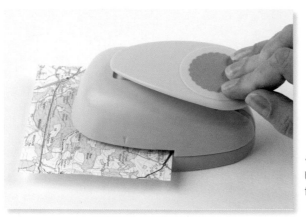

◀ **STEP 1**
Using a scalloped-edge circle punch, cut eight circles from an old paper map.

▲ **STEP 2**
Fold each circle in half, map detail outermost. Ensure you match up the scallops on both curved edges.

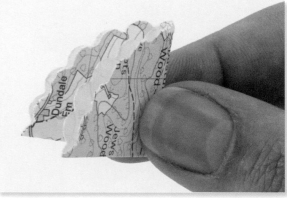

▲ **STEP 3**
Fold each circle in half again along the horizontal edge.

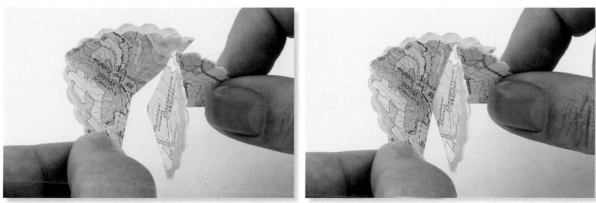

▲ STEP 4

Take up the first shape and open out the last fold made in step 3. Glue in the second shape, halfway between the centre fold and the horizontal crease of the first.

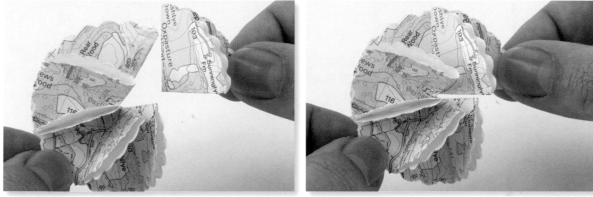

▲ STEP 5

Repeat step 4 to insert five of the remaining six pieces.

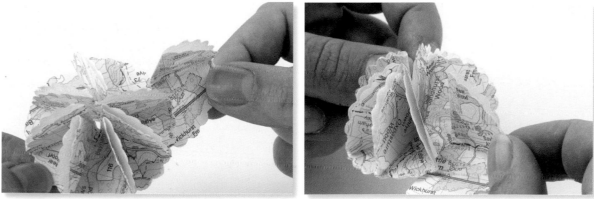

▲ STEP 6

Slot the final piece in place so that the bottom fold slots underneath the next-adjacent piece.

▲ STEP 7

Fold down each upright piece of the flower to create a flat, layered rosette.
Allow the paper to fold down in its natural direction.

▲ STEP 8

Push a brad through the hole in the centre of each
rosette. Set aside.

▲ STEP 9

Cut triangular pennants from orange card. The triangles
should be 130 x 130 x 120mm (5 x 5 x 4¾ in). Trim the
long edges of the pennants with scalloped-edge scissors.
Make sure the scallops line up on either side of the
triangle from the bottom point upwards.

▲ STEP 10

Cut thin stems and leaf shapes out of the map paper for
each pennant of bunting. Glue the stem centrally on to
the pennant. Then glue on the flower, making sure that
the brad lines up with the stem.

▲ STEP 11

Sew the pennants onto a length of co-ordinating ribbon,
at the top corners of each flag. Ensure you leave plenty of
ribbon at either end to be able to secure the bunting once
complete. Sew from the back of the flag to the front, and
attach the thread again at the back.

Rose bouquet

Roses are a classic, romantic flower, and a favourite for weddings, St Valentine's Day and anniversaries. These paper roses are longer-lasting (and more affordable!) than the real thing!

While the folding and turning of the paper strip may prove tricky for beginners, this skill can soon be mastered, and the flowers made in no time. Each flower is formed of a single length of paper, where the width of the paper determines the size of the flower. I have used deep pink paper to create the buds; but yellow or red roses look equally fabulous!

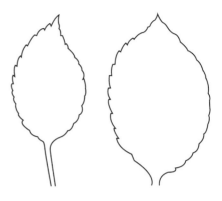

Materials and tools

▷ Basic toolkit (see pages 10–11)
▷ 5 x sheets of deep pink paper, 297 x 210mm (11¾ x 8¼in)
▷ Green card, 300 x 300mm (12 x 12in)
▷ Quilling tool
▷ Floristry wire, green
▷ Bucket, 100mm (4in) high; 100mm (4in) diameter at brim
▷ Floristry oasis, height: 50mm x diameter: 80mm (3⅛ x 2in) (optional)
▷ Floristry tape, green, 10mm (⅜in) wide
▷ Leaf rubber stamp and green ink pad (optional)
▷ Pliers

Templates

These leaf templates are reproduced at three-quarters of actual size. You will need to photocopy or scan them at 133 per cent for the correct size.

Use these templates at step 13 if you do not have a leaf rubber stamp.

▲ **STEP 1**
Cut a sheet of dark pink paper lengthways into strips roughly 30mm (1¼in) wide. Cut a 10 x 20mm (⅜ x ¾in) notch out of one end of your first strip.

▲ **STEP 2**
Insert the cut end of the paper between the prongs of the quilling tool.

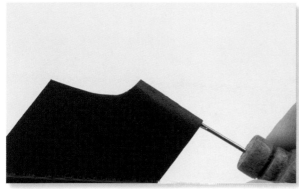

▲ STEP 3

Twisting the tool away from yourself, start to coil the paper until you reach the wider part of the strip.

▲ STEP 4

Fold down the length of paper so that it is at right angles to the tool.

▲ STEP 5

Turn the quilling tool and fold the paper strip upwards as you turn so that it sits horizontally again.

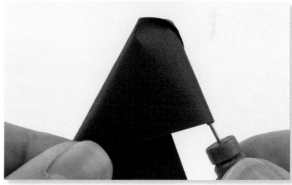

▲ STEP 6

Fold the paper back down at right angles to the tool so that the paper hangs down close to the previous fold. As you continue to fold and turn, space out the folds slightly more each time.

Tip

The roses can be kept as tight buds if the paper coil is not allowed to unwind once the quilling tool is removed.

▲ STEP 7

Once the rose is the required size, remove the quilling tool, holding the rose in one hand. Fold the end down behind the length and loosen the bud slightly.

▲ STEP 8

Glue the end in place. Make more roses in varying sizes using the remaining strips of paper.

▲ **STEP 9**
Take a 150mm (6in) length of floristry wire. Fold over the end of the wire with pliers to make a hook.

▲ **STEP 10**
Feed the wire through the rose so that the hook 'catches' the centre of the flower.

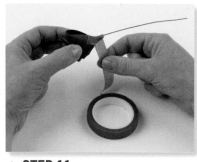

▲ **STEP 11**
Secure the wire to the flower using a strip of floristry tape around the base of the rosebud.

▲ **STEP 12**
Place the floristry oasis into the bucket. Insert the wire of the roses into the oasis so they hold upright. The wire can be trimmed with pliers to change the height of the flowers.

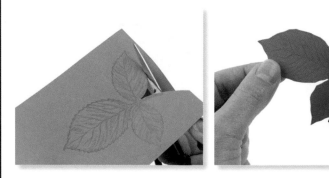

◀ **STEP 13**
Use a rubber stamp and green ink to stamp a leaf pattern onto green card. Cut out the leaves and place them within the arrangement. They can be glued in place if you wish.

The finished bouquet.

Why not make...
a gift box posy

Decorate a 205 x 205mm (8 x 8in) gift box with an arrangement of five roses on the lid, on a base of green leaves. Make the roses, but do not attach floristry wire. Instead, glue the buds together into a tight posy. Smaller roses can also be made and attached to the sides of the gift box.

Christmas wreath

The festive period is the ideal opportunity to get creative and make your own paper-crafted decorations.

This stylish wreath is made from concertina-folded flowers in two shades of green for a subtle colour scheme; however, the concertina flowers can be as brightly coloured as you wish, to keep in with the scheme of your festive decorations.

Note

The number of concertina flowers needed will depend on your wreath size. Here, six large, light green flowers are made with 50mm (2in) wide card and six smaller, dark green flowers made with 40mm (1½in) wide card. Card has been used for this project to make a stronger wreath.

Materials and tools

▷ Basic toolkit (see pages 10–11)
▷ Patterned, double-sided card, two shades of green, 300mm (12in) long
▷ Plain green card, 6 x 6cm (2¼ x 2¼in)
▷ Scoring board and creasing tool
▷ Circle punch, 60mm (2¼in) diameter
▷ Floristry wire circle frame 300mm (12in) diameter
▷ Narrow adhesive tape
▷ 12 x green buttons (6 light green, 6 dark green)
▷ Green embroidery thread
▷ Red ribbon

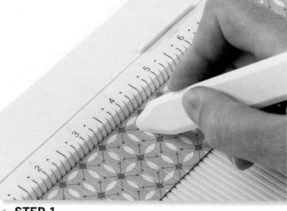

▲ STEP 1

From one sheet of green patterned card, cut strips 40mm (1½in) wide. Place a strip on the scoring board and score lines across the width every 5mm (³/₁₆in) with the tool. Do this for the whole length of the strip of card and repeat for a second strip.

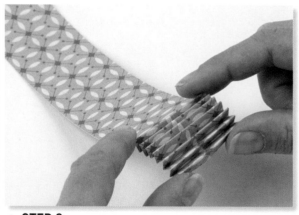

▲ STEP 2

Fold each strip of card back and forth along the score lines to concertina the length.

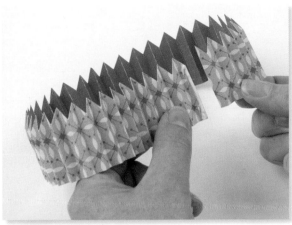

STEP 3

With small sharp scissors, snip the ends of each of the mountain folds, all along one long edge of each strip. You can omit this step for a smoother flower.

STEP 4

Take both ends and glue the strips together to form a ring.

STEP 5

Cut or punch a 60mm (2¼in) diameter circle of green card and dab plenty of PVA glue onto it. Push the concertinaed ring onto the circle of glue so that it lies flat. This takes some patience as the concertinas will 'spring' up and not form a circle. However, by carefully holding the flower with one hand and arranging it with the other hand, it is achievable. Hold the flower in place for a minute, then place a weight on the top of the flower and leave to dry. Repeat steps 1 to 5 with the wider, lighter green card.

STEP 6

Tie green embroidery thread through the button holes, and fasten on the reverse of each button. Dab strong glue on the reverse of each button and attach to the top of a flower. Attach the darker green buttons to the darker card flowers, and the lighter green buttons to the light green card.

▲ STEP 7

Use strips of narrow tape to attach the larger flowers evenly around the edge of the floristry wire circle frame.

▲ STEP 8

Use glue to attach the smaller flowers evenly between, and on top of, the large flowers.

The wreath with flowers in place.

▲ STEP 9

Attach red ribbon, tied in a bow, to the wreath to complete.

Why not make... a greeting card

Make a matching card with two concertina flowers of differing sizes and complementary colours. Place the smaller flower on top of the larger to create added dimension, attach to a card blank and embellish with a punched circle of matching patterned card and a pretty ribbon tie.

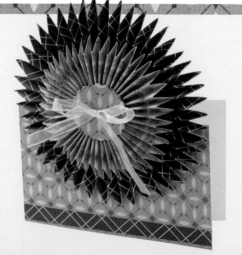

The finished wreath.

Everyday
Thank-you card

Create a greeting card using pretty patterned papers to show your appreciation – it is sure to please its recipient!

This project is ideal for the novice papercrafter, and can be adapted to make matching tags or for decorating gift bags and boxes, using flowers in varying sizes. Here, we use a small, vintage floral pattern to create simple, yet effective, scalloped-edge petals. These petals are then combined to make an attractive rosette.

Materials and tools

▷ Basic toolkit (see pages 10–11)
▷ Floral patterned paper, 200 x 120mm (8 x 4¾in)
▷ Co-ordinating paper, 140 x 120mm (5½ x 4¾in)
▷ Yellow card blank, 170 x 125mm (6¾ x 4⅞in)
▷ Yellow card, 200 x 120mm (8 x 4¾in)
▷ Blue brad, 7mm (¼in) diameter
▷ Die-cutting tool with scalloped-edge circle die, 50mm (2in) diameter
▷ Scalloped-edge scissors

STEP 1

Using the die-cutting tool and a scalloped-edge circle die, cut six circles from floral patterned paper 50mm (2in) in diameter.

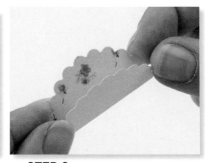

STEP 2

Fold each circle in half, pattern innermost. Try to fold the circle so that the scallops on both curved edges line up. Use a bone folder to give a neat crease on the folded edge.

STEP 3

Hold the shape with the straight edge vertical and the scallop edge uppermost. Count three scallops in from the left corner, then fold the top layer back towards you from this point, to reveal the patterned paper and create a petal. Fold all six circles in this way.

STEP 4

Cut a yellow scallop-edged circle 50mm (2in) diameter. Mark the centre of the circle with a pencil dot and, applying your glue sparingly, attach one folded shape to this. Ensure that the fold made in step 3 leads into the centre of the circle, and that the petal is outermost.

▲ **STEP 5**

Clue a second petal so that it tucks in to the first. Continue glueing the petals in this way until all six are in place.

▲ **STEP 6**

Pierce the centre of the flower with a needle tool and insert a blue brad. Spread out the wings of the brad on the reverse side of the flower.

◀ **STEP 7**

Trim the short edges of the sheet of co-ordinating patterned paper with scalloped-edge scissors, and attach to the yellow card blank. Then glue a yellow card circle 100mm (4in) diameter to this. Finally, attach the flower to the yellow circle.

The finished card.

Why not make... a gift tag

These smaller petals are made with a scallop circle 30mm (1¼in) in diameter; however, the flower is constructed in the same way as in the main project.

Upcycled book flower

Upcycling is very much in fashion; it is fun to make something new from an older object that may have otherwise been discarded.

We might find a second-hand book in a charity shop that may never be read again – so why not use the pages for another purpose?

Materials and tools

▷ Basic toolkit (see pages 10–11)
▷ Old book
▷ Die-cutting tool with circle die, 60mm (2¼in) diameter
▷ Ink pad, pink
▷ Clean piece of sponge
▷ Pink gem stones, 3mm (⅛in) diameter
▷ Scrap paper

Tips

- The pages do not have to be inked and can be left plain if you wish.
- You can upcycle other papers such as old maps, wrapping paper or sheet music in the same way.

▲ STEP 1
Using the die-cutting tool, cut six circles from the pages of the book. Fold each circle in half, keeping the text reading upright on the outside.

▲ STEP 2
Rest each semi-circle on scrap paper. Ink the curved edge with a sponge dabbed in pink ink. Allow to dry.

▲ STEP 3
Keeping the inked edge outermost, fold each circle in half again, curve to curve, to form a quarter circle.

▲ STEP 4
Unfold the shape to a semi-circle and hold it with the inked side facing away from you. With the folded edge uppermost, fold the left corner upwards so part of the curved edge is in line with the centre fold line.

▲ STEP 5
Now fold the right corner point over in the same way, to overlap the curved edge on the left. This will form an inverted triangle shape, with two corner points uppermost.

▲ STEP 6

Working one by one, glue the six petals, point innermost, to form a neat circle on the lid of the box.

▲ STEP 7

Using tweezers, attach a small pink gem stone to the centre to finish.

Why not make... place cards

For place cards, make smaller flowers with 40mm (1½in) diameter cut circles. Fold and ink the papers in the same way as in the main project, and mount the flowers onto pink card 100 x 100mm (4 x 4in) that has been scored and folded in half.

Yellow flower noteblock

The historic art of paper-folding was further evolved into 'teabag folding' by Tiny van der Plas in Holland over twenty years ago. Van der Plas folded teabag wrappers and slotted them together to form rosettes. Since then, the idea of arranging identically folded squares of paper has become popular as the easy folding technique garners stylish results.

Here, we fold squares of colourful patterned paper in a set sequence, then arrange the petals to form a rosette. This bright, colourful noteblock would make a lovely present for somebody starting a new job.

The finished noteblock.

Materials and tools

▷ Basic toolkit (see pages 10–11)
▷ Patterned paper, 300 x 300mm (12 x 12in)
▷ Blank white noteblock, 85 x 85mm x 30mm (3¼ x 3¼ x 1¼in)
▷ Turquoise card, 205 x 95mm (8 x 3¾in)
▷ Red brad, 3mm (⅛in) diameter
▷ Corner rounder punch (optional)

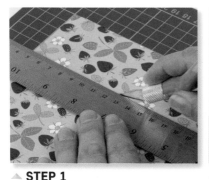

▲ STEP 1
From the patterned paper, cut out eight squares, each 50 x 50mm (2 x 2in).

▲ STEP 2
Fold each square, edge to edge, with the pattern innermost. Crease along the fold with your fingers.

▲ STEP 3
Open out the square of paper. With the pattern outermost, fold the paper corner to corner and crease.

STEP 4
Open out the paper again and fold diagonally to match up the other two corners.

STEP 5
Open the shape slightly so that you see three crease lines.

STEP 6
Push the sides of the shape inwards to form a triangular 'hat' shape.

STEP 7
Each resultant shape has four 'points' at the base. Fold the front left point downwards, towards the centre line of the triangle.

STEP 8
Fold down the front right point in the same way. Repeat the process from step 2 onwards for the remaining seven squares of paper.

a   b   c

STEP 9
Hold one shape with the point facing downwards. Dab a little PVA glue on the exposed right-hand edge. Slot a second shape into the first as shown in the sequence above. Marry the edge of the second piece with the centre crease of the first.

STEP 10
Slot each piece under the next in this way, and glue in place, forming a rosette.

▶ STEP 11
Ensure that the folded-down points of the final piece tuck over the edges of the two shapes on either side. Set aside while the glue dries.

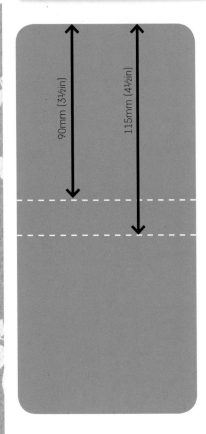

90mm (3½in)

115mm (4½in)

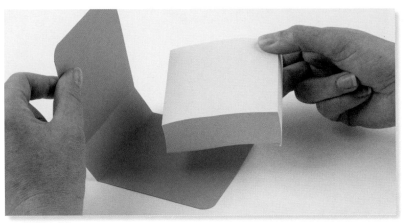

▲ STEP 12
Round all four corners of the turquoise card. Score a line at 90mm (3½in) from a short edge. Then at 115mm (4½in) fold the card over and use a bone folder to make a strong crease (see diagram, left). Apply PVA glue to the inside 'spine' of the turquoise card cover. Insert the plain noteblock and secure to the cover with glue.

▲ STEP 13
Add the red brad to the centre of the flower, and glue the flower to the cover of the noteblock.

Tip
A pad of sticky notes can be used inside the card cover, instead of a white paper block.

Why not make... a greeting card

For a matching card, attach three folded flowers in contrasting colours to a card blank for a striking floral display.

Make the flowers from 40 x 40mm (1½ x 1½in) squares, folded in the same sequence as shown in steps 2 to 11. Push a brad through the centre of each flower and mount them onto a rectangle of card. Attach a strip of matching patterned paper to a pink card blank 110 x 180mm (4¼ x 7in). Finally, attach the flowers to the card with glue.

Pinwheel napkin rings

Spinning pinwheels, powered by the wind, are often a feature of the seaside or a garden party celebration. In this project, we create a floral variation on the traditional pinwheel to create two unique napkin rings.

Whilst the pinwheels may look intricate, they are surprisingly easy to construct, and do not require many materials.

The finished napkin ring.

Materials and tools

▷ Basic toolkit (see pages 10–11)
▷ Double-sided patterned card, 305 x 305mm (12 x 12in)
▷ Light green brad, 3mm (⅛in) diameter
▷ Needle tool
▷ Plain card (for templates)

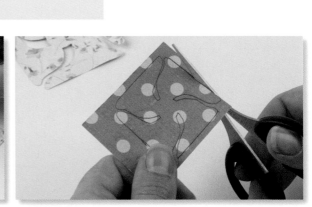

▲ STEP 1

Trace the large and small pinwheel templates from page 84 onto plain card. Place the large pinwheel template onto patterned card and draw around it with a pencil. Then flip over the template and draw a second, 'reversed' shape next to the first. Draw around the small pinwheel template once.

▲ STEP 2

Cut out the three shapes from the patterned card.

▶ STEP 3

Place the shapes on a cutting mat. Use a needle tool to prick holes in the ends of each leg. Then pierce a hole in the centre of each shape. Make sure that the hole is large enough for the wings of a brad to pass through.

STEP 4

Take up one of the large shapes. Carefully lift one end of a leg and fold it into the centre. Glue in place so that the pierced holes line up.

STEP 5

Fold each remaining log over in this way and glue in place. Repeat with the small shape. Then repeat for the other large shape, but fold with the reverse side uppermost.

STEP 6

Layer the large pinwheels, alternating the patterns as shown. Dab glue onto the reverse of the centre of the topmost pinwheel to attach it to the one beneath.

STEP 7

Attach the small pinwheel on top to form a flower. Thread a brad through the centre of all three pinwheels. Spread the wings of the brad out flat on the underside of the pinwheel flower.

STEP 8

Cut a 20mm (1in) wide strip of the patterned card and roll into a hoop around a glue stick container or similar tubular object. Glue the ends together.

STEP 9

Finally, attach the rolled-up hoop to the pinwheel flower with glue. Make a second napkin ring, changing the order of the layered pinwheels for interest.

Templates

These templates are reproduced at actual size.

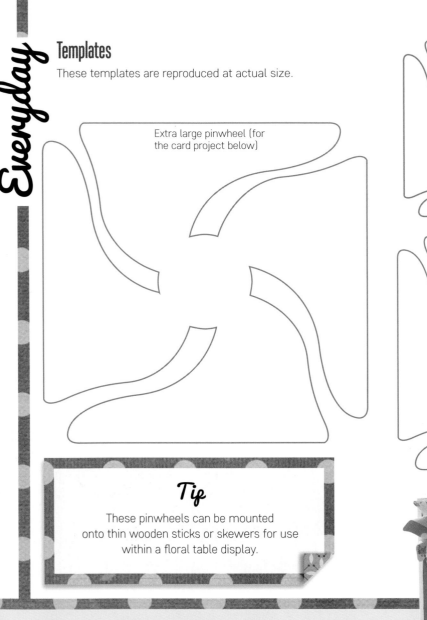

Small pinwheel

Extra large pinwheel (for the card project below)

Large pinwheel

Tip

These pinwheels can be mounted onto thin wooden sticks or skewers for use within a floral table display.

Why not make... a greeting card

Make a three-dimensional greeting card with two-layer pinwheels, using all three templates above. Cut out and construct the shapes as before, following steps 1 to 6. Insert a brad into the centre of each pinwheel, mount the pinwheels on a rectangle of pink card before attaching to a white card blank 178 x 126mm (7 x 5in).

Three-dimensional cards will get crushed unless they are hand delivered, so package your card inside a small box to protect it. Ready-made card boxes can be purchased for this purpose.

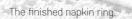
The finished napkin ring.

Floral pencil pot

Enhance any desk with a decorated pencil pot, adorned with a pretty flower made of four individual layers. The blue and brown colour combination brings calm to a working environment and cheer to the working day.

The flowers are made from brown handmade paper printed with a white pattern on one side. Each flower shape is cut by hand and the ends pinched, then the layers built up, with a large brad as a flower centre.

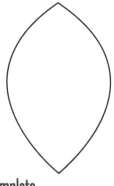

Template

This template is reproduced at actual size.

Materials and tools

▷ Basic toolkit (see pages 10–11)
▷ Sheet of brown handmade paper, ideally with pattern on one side
▷ Blank pencil pot, 90 x 90mm (3½ x 3½in)
▷ 4 x cream brads, each 6mm (¼in) diameter
▷ Plain card for template
▷ Strong glue

Tip

Strong paper is best for this project. Handmade paper can withstand a lot of handling and manipulation.

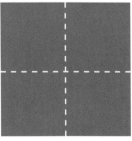

▲ **STEP 1**

Cut out sixteen pieces of brown paper, each 70mm (2¾in) square. Fold each square in half horizontally, pattern innermost, and then in half again.

▲ **STEP 2**

Make a guide from plain card using the petal template above. Place the guide on one folded piece with the point in the folded corner, and draw around it with a pencil.

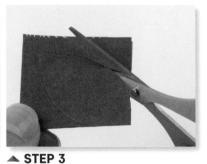

▲ **STEP 3**

Cut out the four-layer petal, but do not cut the petal point away from the corner of the paper. This will keep all the petals together.

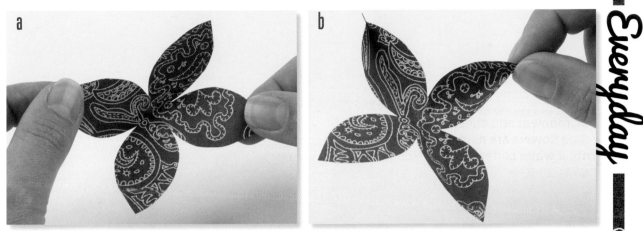

a

b

▲ **STEP 4**

Open out one shape, pattern side up, and pinch the petal end. Put a tiny dot of glue
inside the very end and hold in place for a few seconds whilst the glue dries.
Repeat for three more layers: pinch and glue two petals with the pattern uppermost,
and one with the pattern face down.

◀ **STEP 6**

Prick a hole in the centre of each
flower layer using a needle tool.
Insert a brad through the centre
of all the layers and spread the
wings out on the reverse side of
the flower.

▲ **STEP 5**

Layer and glue the petals together as
follows, alternating the position
of the petal points:
a) Glue two layers together, pattern
    side **up**.
b) Glue one layer on top, pattern
    side **down**.
c) Glue a final layer on top, pattern
    side **up**.
Repeat for all flowers.

▶ **STEP 7**
Glue one flower to each side of the
pencil pot using strong glue.

87

The finished pencil pot.

Why not make... a sticky-note holder

Make a layered, pinched flower in the same manner as shown in the
main project, to sit atop a pad of useful sticky notes.
Use the instructions for folding the noteblock cover on page 80 as a basis
for creating the cover of the sticky-note holder.

Purple flower card

These deep purple flowers make a cheerful and unique greeting card for anyone fond of a bold, bright design!

Whilst the petals do fold flat, they also stand proud to create a three-dimensional border around the centres, recreating the layers of a flower.

The purple and green colour scheme harmonises to give this card a pleasing overall effect.

Materials and tools

▷ Basic toolkit (see pages 10–11)
▷ Purple, double-sided patterned card, 305 x 305mm (12 x 12in)
▷ Handmade, double-sided green patterned paper, 110 x 160mm (4¼ x 6¼in)
▷ Plain green card
▷ Yellow card blank, 130 x 180mm (5 x 7in)
▷ Circle punch, 16mm (½in) diameter
▷ 3 x purple buttons, 10mm (½in) diameter
▷ Purple sewing thread
▷ Sewing needle

Template

This template is reproduced at actual size. The dashed lines indicate where to fold the petal at step 2.

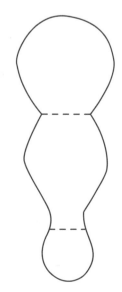

The finished card.

▲ STEP 1

Each of the three flowers is formed of five petals – draw around the petal template on page 90 fifteen times onto purple card, with pencil. Cut out these shapes carefully.

▲ STEP 2

Fold each petal shape gently where indicated on the template opposite, up and then down.

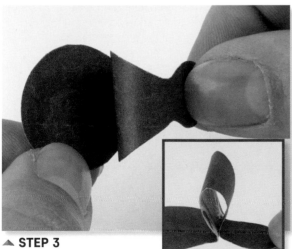

▲ STEP 3

Dab a small amount of glue inside the folds. Pinch the folds together to make a loop (see inset). Keep the flat ends level with each other. Repeat steps 2 to 3 for five petals.

▲ STEP 4

Dab glue on the narrow end of one petal. Arrange a second petal at an angle, with the narrow end overlapping the first. Glue the second petal in place.

▲ STEP 5

Apply glue to the narrow end of the second petal, and attach the third, and so on, until you have a full flower of five petals. Set aside to let the glue dry. Meanwhile, repeat steps 3 to 5 to make two more flowers.

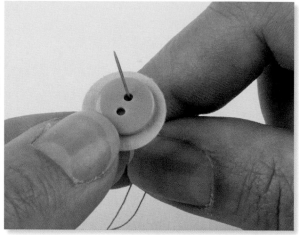

▲ STEP 6

Punch three 16mm (½in) circles from the green card. Use a needle and a double length of purple sewing thread to attach each button to a card circle. Tie off the thread on the reverse of the paper circle. Trim off any excess thread.

▲ STEP 7

Glue the button, on the card, into the centre of each flower.

▲ STEP 8

Mount a rectangle of purple card onto the yellow card blank and attach the green patterned paper to this. Now attach the three flowers to the green paper by dabbing small amounts of glue under each petal.

Why not make... a gift tag

The flower on this gift tag is made in a nearly identical manner
to those on the card, with a brad in the centre instead of a button
to hold the flower in place on the tag.

Raised flower card

The papercrafting world is full of beautiful co-ordinating patterned papers that cry out to be made into flowers.

The classic blue and white colour scheme is used here to create a design reminiscent of quilting and fabric patterns. The flower comprises eight rectangles of folded card, in alternating colours. With folding, the ends of the petals stand away from the card, adding further dimension and interest to the design.

The finished card.

Materials and tools

▷ Basic toolkit (see pages 10–11)
▷ Patterned paper, blue: 300 x 300mm (12 x 12in)
▷ Patterned paper, white (with contrasting pattern): 300 x 300mm (12 x 12in)
▷ Blue card, 110 x 110mm (4¼ x 4¼in)
▷ 2 x circle punches: 16mm (½in), 25mm (¾in)
▷ Die-cutting tool with circle die, 40mm (1½in) diameter
▷ White card blank, 145 x 145mm (5¾ x 5¾in)
▷ Adhesive foam pad

▲ STEP 1
Cut four pieces of blue patterned paper, each 40 x 60mm (1½ x 2¼in). Cut four pieces at the same size from white paper with a blue pattern.

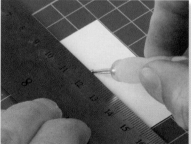

▲ STEP 2
Score each of the rectangles in half lengthways.

▲ STEP 3
Holding the shape with the pattern facing away from you, fold each corner in towards the centre score line.

◀ **STEP 4**

Fold the bottom right corner up to meet the centre score line. Fold down the top right corner in the same way. You will now have a kite shape (see inset).

▲ **STEP 5**

Fold the wider (top) point over to create a flat edge, but do not fold down the point completely.
Repeat steps 3 to 5 for the remaining seven shapes.

▲ **STEP 6**

Punch a circle of blue card 40mm (1½in) diameter. Attach all the petals to the card circle with the fine points inwards. The petals should touch on either side but should not overlap.

▲ **STEP 7**

Punch one 25mm (1in) circle from the white patterned paper and one 16mm (½in) circle from the blue paper. Glue to the centre of the flower.

◀ **STEP 8**

Attach the flower to a square of blue card (cut to 110 x 110mm/4¼ x 4¼in), using an adhesive foam pad. Raise the points of the petals so that the flower stands proud of the card. Mount onto two layered squares of the patterned paper (white paper cut to 135 x 135mm/5¼ x 5¼in; blue paper cut to 145 x 145mm/5¾ x 5¾in). Finally, attach all elements with double-sided tape to the white card blank.

INDEX